HOT LAVA!

CONTENTS

make believe ideas

WHAT IS A VOLCANO?

A volcano is an opening in the Earth's surface where hot, liquid rock can escape. An erupting volcano is a type of **natural disaster**—a major event caused by the natural processes of the Earth. Other natural disasters include floods, hurricanes, tornadoes, **earthquakes**, and **tsunamis**.

DID YOU KNOW?

Lightning can be seen in a volcanic ash cloud. It happens when particles collide and create an electrical charge.

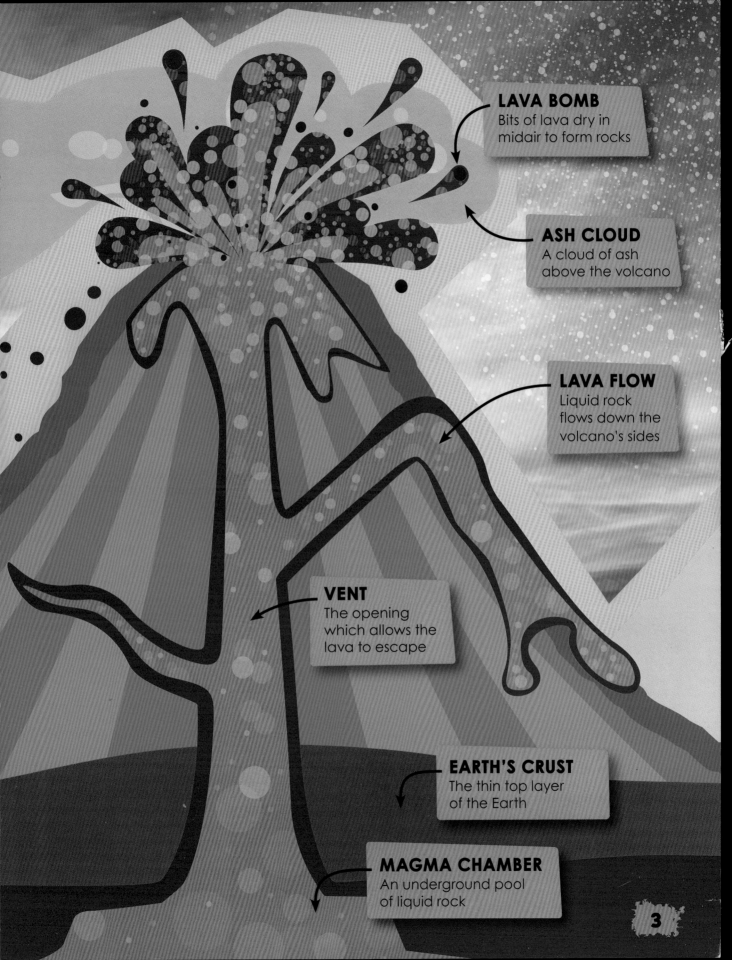

LAVA BOMB
Bits of lava dry in
midair to form rocks

ASH CLOUD
A cloud of ash
above the volcano

LAVA FLOW
Liquid rock
flows down the
volcano's sides

VENT
The opening
which allows the
lava to escape

EARTH'S CRUST
The thin top layer
of the Earth

MAGMA CHAMBER
An underground pool
of liquid rock

VOLCANO VARIETIES

Volcanoes come in a variety of shapes and sizes. There are four main types and each has its own unique features.

CINDER CONES

The smallest and most common volcanoes. They look like upside-down ice-cream cones. They are made of cooled bits of **lava** called cinders.

Cerro Negro in Nicaragua is the Earth's most **active cinder cone**. It has erupted more than 20 times since 1850, most recently in 1999.

STRATOVOLCANOES

Stratovolcanoes are steep-sided cones built of many layers of lava and ash, caused by eruptions.

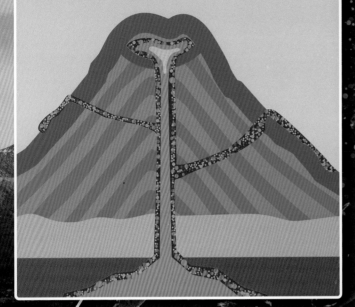

Erta Ale in Ethiopia is an active shield volcano with two bubbling lava lakes at the top.

SHIELD

These giant volcanoes with gentle slopes look like an ancient warrior's **shield**. They are made of lots of layers of lava that has oozed out and cooled to form hard rock.

Mount Etna is Europe's tallest active stratovolcano. It is found on the island of Sicily in Italy.

CALDERA

Caldera is the name for the huge crater formed when the top of a stratovolcano collapses inside itself.

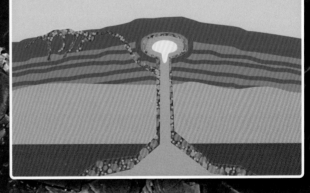

Diamond Head, a giant caldera on Hawaii, was given its name by British sailors who discovered sparkling volcanic crystals in the sand and thought they were diamonds.

FAMOUS ERUPTIONS:
KRAKATOA

A volcano on the island of Krakatoa in Indonesia erupted in 1883, causing two-thirds of the island to collapse into a **caldera**. It created a series of landslides and **tsunamis** that killed more than 36,000 people.

TSUNAMIS

The explosion created tsunamis; enormous waves that were caused by fast-moving clouds of gas and volcanic matter entering the sea. These waves spread across the Indian Ocean, wiping out coastal towns and cities.

WHAT'S THAT SOUND?
Krakatoa's eruptions were so loud that they were heard 1,930 miles (3,110 km) away in Perth, Australia.

WORLDWIDE EFFECTS
Krakatoa's eruption was so powerful that it changed the world's climate. Large amounts of sulfur dioxide were shot into the atmosphere, cooling the whole planet. In the Northern Hemisphere, temperatures fell by 0.72 °F (0.4 °C).

WHY DO VOLCANOES ERUPT?

The **Earth's crust** is made up of huge slabs called **tectonic plates**. These fit together like a jigsaw puzzle, but they can move. Sometimes when these plates rub against each other or pull apart, they can cause volcanic eruptions.

PLATE MOVEMENT

A convergent plate is one that pushes against another. Sometimes one plate will slide under the other, forming a mountain or volcano. Divergent is when two plates are pulling apart, creating a rift.

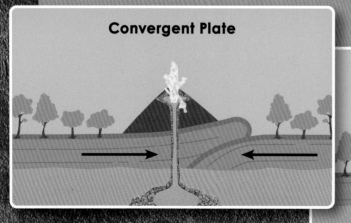

Convergent Plate

Divergent Plate

MAIN TYPES OF ERUPTION

EXPLOSIVE
Some eruptions can be explosive, blasting **lava** high into the sky.

EFFUSIVE
Other eruptions are calmer, with gentle lava flows.

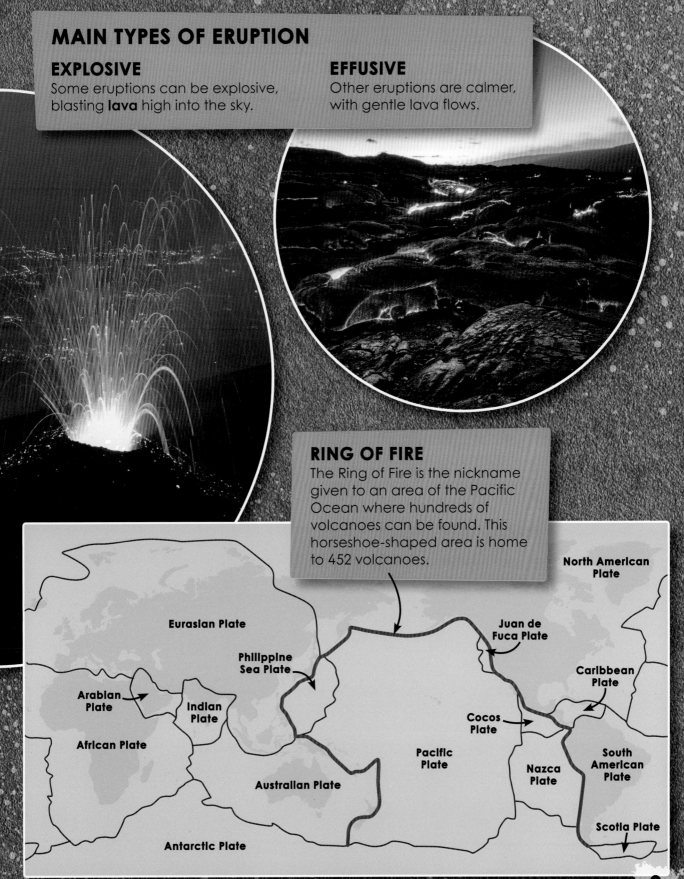

RING OF FIRE
The Ring of Fire is the nickname given to an area of the Pacific Ocean where hundreds of volcanoes can be found. This horseshoe-shaped area is home to 452 volcanoes.

North American Plate

Eurasian Plate

Juan de Fuca Plate

Philippine Sea Plate

Caribbean Plate

Arabian Plate

Indian Plate

Cocos Plate

African Plate

Pacific Plate

South American Plate

Nazca Plate

Australian Plate

Antarctic Plate

Scotia Plate

LIFE CYCLE OF A VOLCANO

Volcanoes move through three stages: **active**, **dormant**, and **extinct**. There are thousands of volcanoes all over the world, all at different stages in their life cycles. The time they stay in each stage varies.

ACTIVE

A volcano that has erupted at least once in the last 10,000 years is called active. It could be erupting now or getting ready to erupt again.

Active magma chamber

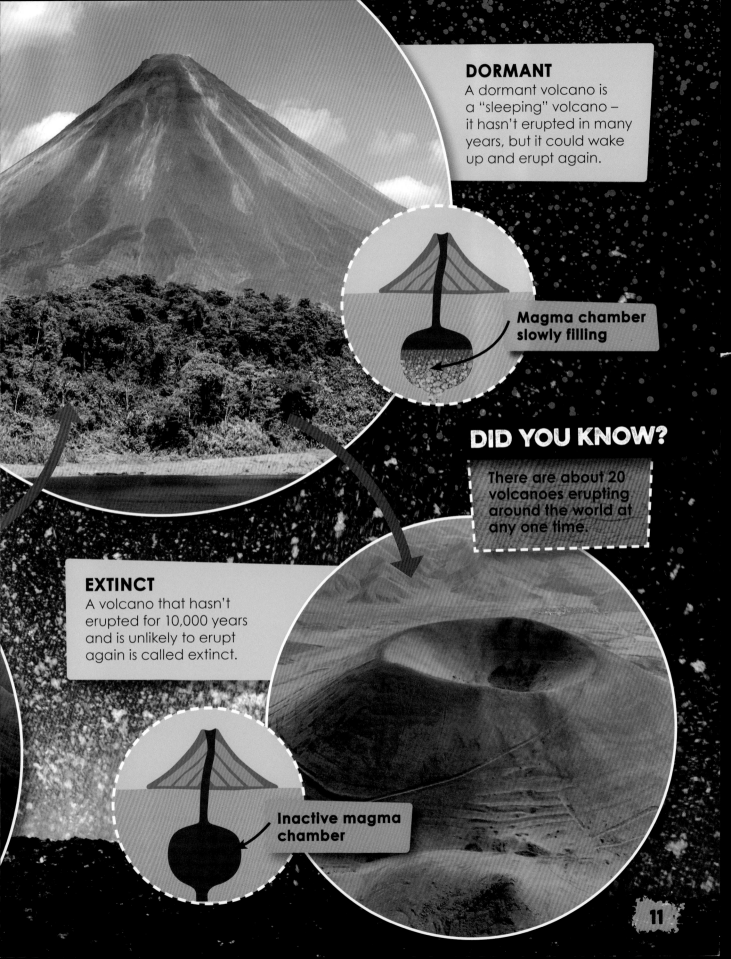

DORMANT

A dormant volcano is a "sleeping" volcano – it hasn't erupted in many years, but it could wake up and erupt again.

Magma chamber slowly filling

DID YOU KNOW?

There are about 20 volcanoes erupting around the world at any one time.

EXTINCT

A volcano that hasn't erupted for 10,000 years and is unlikely to erupt again is called extinct.

Inactive magma chamber

11

FAMOUS ERUPTIONS:
MOUNT VESUVIUS

The eruption of Mount Vesuvius in Italy is one of the most famous volcanic explosions of all time. It erupted in AD 79, covering the cities of Pompeii and Herculaneum in a thick layer of ash. It happened so suddenly that many people were buried alive in the blast.

PERFECTLY PRESERVED
Scientists dug up Pompeii and Herculaneum in the early 18th century. The layers of ash, mud, and rubble had protected the buildings.

Scientists found this 2000-year-old loaf of bread at Pompeii. It had turned to charcoal.

Plaster casts of bodies in Pompeii show what people were doing when the eruption happened.

LIQUID ROCK

When molten **magma** bursts out of a volcano, it becomes **lava**. Sometimes this liquid rock pops and explodes into the air. Other times it flows out of the mountain like a red-hot river. Scientists call fiery explosions of **lava bombs** and cinders **Strombolian** eruptions.

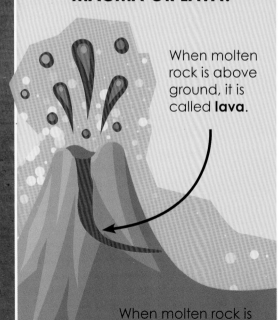

MAGMA OR LAVA?

When molten rock is above ground, it is called **lava**.

When molten rock is below ground, it is called **magma**.

When lava cools, it hardens into solid rock. New land is created.

Sometimes liquid lava flows away, leaving a hard crust. This creates a **lava cave**.

In time, plants grow on the volcanic rock. It becomes a home for living things.

DID YOU KNOW?

Lava can reach a deadly 2000°F (1100°C). That's over ten times as hot as a boiling kettle!

2000°F (1100°C)

HOT WATER

In volcanic areas, **magma** under the ground heats nearby water. If this water reaches Earth's surface, it forms **geothermal** hot springs. Most pools are boiling hot, but some are cool enough for bathing.

At Hot Water Beach in New Zealand, swimmers dig their own hot pools. The sea water cools hot spring water, making it perfect for a soak.

Snow monkeys enjoy warming up in this natural hot spring in Japan.

This hot spring in Yellowstone National Park is more than 120 feet (36 meters) deep. That's about as deep as an eight-story building.

Strokkur **geyser** in Iceland erupts about every eight minutes. Underground water flows onto magma and then boils and bursts out of the ground.

DID YOU KNOW?

Every continent in the world has geothermal pools, even Antarctica.

17

FAMOUS ERUPTIONS:
MOUNT ST. HELENS

Mount St. Helens, a **stratovolcano** in Washington, USA, erupted on May 18, 1980. It was the biggest volcanic explosion in US history. Altogether, 57 people were killed and 250 houses were flattened, along with 47 bridges, 15 miles (24 km) of railways, and 185 miles (298 km) of highway.

GETTING READY TO ERUPT

From mid-March 1980, the area around Mount St. Helens shook with up to 200 **earthquakes** a day. Experts monitored the volcano, and people living within five miles of it were moved away for safety.

AVALANCHE
During the blast, the whole north side of the volcano collapsed, causing a huge debris avalanche. This mixed with ice, snow, and water, creating large mudflows that flattened more than 10 million trees.

AGAINST THE ODDS
Some small plants that were buried in winter snow when the blast happened survived. Their roots were protected by the snow and soil.

ASH AND DUST

Erupting volcanoes can shoot enormous clouds of dust and ash into the sky. The ash is formed from tiny pieces of volcanic rock and can travel large distances, carried by the wind. It can also change the weather conditions.

After the 1815 explosion of Mount Tambora in Indonesia, ash particles blocked out the sunlight in parts of Europe and lowered the temperature. People called 1816 the Year-Without-a-Summer.

The 2010 eruption of Eyjafjallajökull in Iceland created an ash cloud so large that airplanes were not allowed to fly across Europe for five days. The cloud was over 5 miles (8 km) high.

Mount Pinatubo, a **stratovolcano** in the Philippines, erupted in 1991. Large clouds of ash shot into the air, blocking out the sunlight for days. The eruption caused the central cone to collapse, leaving a **caldera**.

GAS AND LIGHTNING

An erupting volcano can release deadly gases and make its own lightning. A volcanic gas cloud can contain gases such as carbon dioxide, carbon monoxide, hydrogen sulfide, and sulfur dioxide. These gases can suffocate or poison people and animals, and even burn through clothes.

DID YOU KNOW?

More than 1,700 people and 3,500 cows were killed at Lake Nyos, a crater lake in West Africa, by a sudden release of carbon dioxide in August 1986.

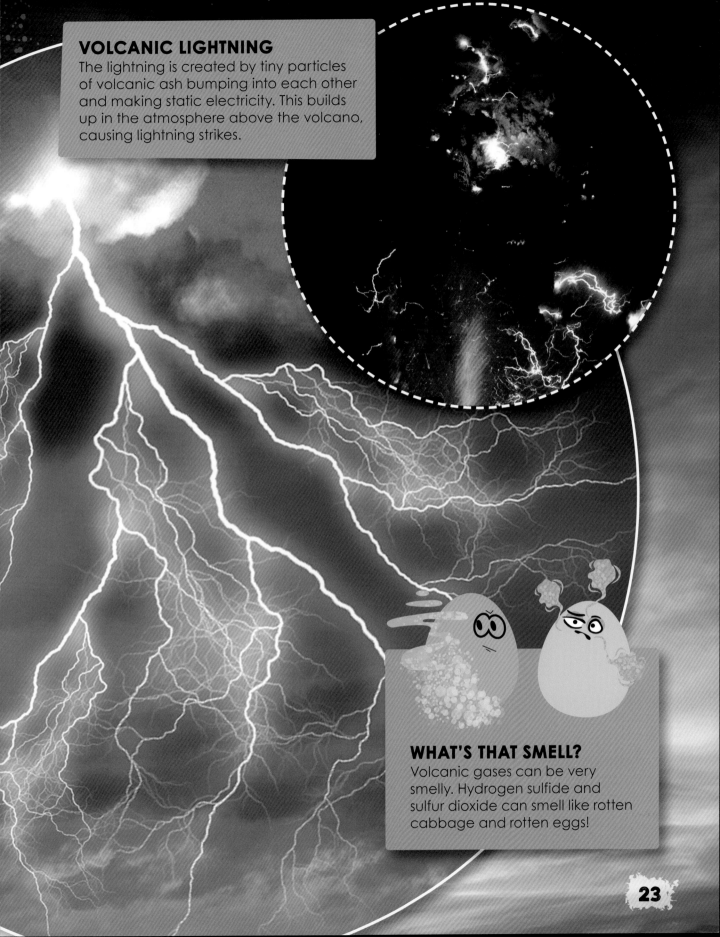

VOLCANIC LIGHTNING

The lightning is created by tiny particles of volcanic ash bumping into each other and making static electricity. This builds up in the atmosphere above the volcano, causing lightning strikes.

WHAT'S THAT SMELL?

Volcanic gases can be very smelly. Hydrogen sulfide and sulfur dioxide can smell like rotten cabbage and rotten eggs!

FAMOUS ERUPTIONS:
ST. PIERRE

The 1902 eruption of Mount Pelée on the Caribbean island of Martinique was one of the worst volcanic disasters in history. On May 8, 1902, the city of St. Pierre was surrounded by a cloud of deadly gas that killed 29,000 people in minutes.

WARNING SIGNS
In the weeks before the eruption, the volcano was showing signs that it was going to blow. Steam and ash were coming out of its **vents**, and there were some land tremors.

The explosion left the city of St. Pierre and its buildings in ruins.

The port at St. Pierre before disaster struck.

MELTED OBJECTS
The heat from the blast was so intense that it melted glass and metal objects in its path, including wine bottles and doorknobs.

WEATHER WARNING

Erupting volcanoes can trigger other **natural disasters** including **tsunamis**, flash floods, **earthquakes**, **mudflows**, **avalanches**, and rockfalls. They can also change the temperature and climate of the earth in the weeks and months after an explosion.

MUDFLOWS

After a volcano explodes, a mix of ash, rocks, and water can sweep down its sides to the towns and villages around it. People and buildings in its path could drown or be crushed by the weight and speed of the mud.

LOCAL WEATHER
The areas around the volcano can experience dark days, heavy rain, and strong winds for months following an eruption.

EARTHQUAKES
The movement of liquid **magma** underneath the volcano can cause an earthquake. It can often cause the land around it to buckle and crack.

SUPERVOLCANOES

Volcanoes with the biggest eruptions are named **supervolcanoes**. Their eruptions can change the landscape and climate of the world.

KEY

1 Bennett Lake, Canada
2 Yellowstone, USA
3 Valles Caldera, USA
4 La Garita Caldera, USA
5 Long Valley Caldera, USA
6 Cerro Galán, Argentina
7 Pastos Grandes, Bolivia
8 Pacana Caldera, Chile
9 The Campi Flegrei, Italy
10 Lake Toba, Indonesia
11 Mount Tambora, Indonesia
12 Baekdu Mountain, North Korea/China
13 Aira Caldera, Japan
14 Kyushu, Japan
15 Mount Iō, Japan
16 Kamchatka, Russia
17 Kurile Lake, Russia
18 Taupo, New Zealand

NORTH AMERICA

SOUTH AMERICA

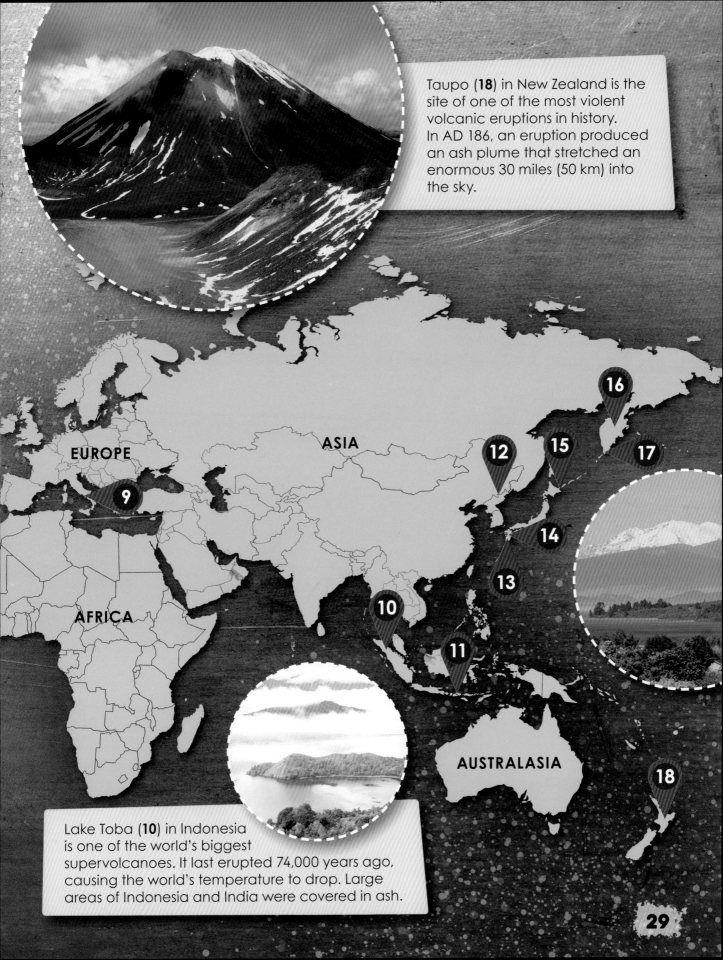

Taupo (**18**) in New Zealand is the site of one of the most violent volcanic eruptions in history. In AD 186, an eruption produced an ash plume that stretched an enormous 30 miles (50 km) into the sky.

EUROPE

ASIA

AFRICA

AUSTRALASIA

Lake Toba (**10**) in Indonesia is one of the world's biggest supervolcanoes. It last erupted 74,000 years ago, causing the world's temperature to drop. Large areas of Indonesia and India were covered in ash.

VOLCANOES IN SPACE

Volcanoes aren't just found on Earth, they have also been seen on other planets and moons in the solar system. They have been discovered using space probes. Many of these volcanoes have been **extinct** for millions of years, but some are still **active**.

VENUS

Venus has more than a thousand volcanoes on its surface. Scientists think that some of them are still active.

MARS

The largest volcano in the solar system, Olympus Mons, can be found on Mars. It is 373 miles (600 km) across and 16 miles (25 km) high.

Scientists have found hundreds of active volcanoes on Jupiter's moon, Io.

VOYAGER

Two Voyager spacecrafts were launched in 1977. They flew past Jupiter's moon Io in 1979. They found around 200 **calderas** and 8 erupting volcanoes.

LIVING ON A VOLCANO

Volcanoes aren't all bad news—some communities and animals rely on them for survival. Soil near volcanoes can be rich in minerals and great for farming. **Geothermal** power, which comes from the heat inside the earth, is a **renewable energy** source that can power homes and factories. Some animals even make their homes in the hot, volcanic soil.

MALEO BIRDS

Maleo birds use heat from volcanoes to hatch their eggs. They bury the eggs in the soil near to volcanoes. When the chicks hatch, they claw their way up to the surface.

EXTINCT VOLCANO

Chu Dang Ya is an **extinct** volcano in Vietnam. Its rich soil is perfect for growing vegetables, such as corn and sweet potatoes, and beautiful flowers.

350 million people, or one in 20 people, in the world live within "danger range" of an active volcano.

The city of Petropavlovsk-Kamchatsky in Russia is overlooked by two enormous **active** volcanoes, Koryaksky and Avachinsky.

The Krafla geothermal power plant, which is located close to the Krafla volcano, is Iceland's biggest power station.

VISIT A VOLCANO

Volcanoes are fascinating natural attractions. It's no wonder that so many people want to visit them. Some of the most famous ones have visitor centers, cable cars, and even helicopters, which allow you to explore the volcano and the area around it.

YELLOWSTONE NATIONAL PARK, USA

Yellowstone National Park in Wyoming sits on an active **supervolcano**. The heat beneath it creates many interesting hydrothermal features – including **geysers, fumaroles**, hot springs, and bubbling mud pools.

SAKURAJIMA, JAPAN

Sakurajima, which means "cherry blossom island" in Japanese, rises dramatically out of the ocean. An **active** volcano, it smokes constantly, and small eruptions happen every day.

TEIDE, TENERIFE
Mount Teide is an active volcano on Tenerife in the Canary Islands. It is the highest point in Spain and one of the most visited natural attractions there. You can reach the top via an eight-minute cable car ride.

MOUNT ETNA, ITALY
Mount Etna on the island of Sicily is one of the most active volcanoes in the world. To get up close to the action, you can hike or take a cable car to the summit. There is even a railway line that circles the base.

MAKE YOUR OWN VOLCANO

Want to witness a volcanic eruption in your own home? Follow the simple instructions below to create your own mini volcano and watch it explode!

YOU WILL NEED:

 baking sheet

 playdough or sand

 baking soda

 vinegar

 red food coloring

 plastic spoons

 small measuring cup

1 On your baking sheet, make a small mountain out of playdough (or sand) and use your thumb to create an indent at the top. This will be your volcano.

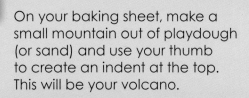

2 Use a small spoon to put about one teaspoon of baking soda into the top of the volcano.

4 Observe the chemical reaction and describe what you see!

3 Add a few drops of red food coloring to a small cup of vinegar. Slowly pour the mixture into the top of your volcano, onto the baking soda.

GLOSSARY

active   used to describe a volcano that is erupting now or has erupted in the last 10,000 years

avalanche   a large mass of snow, ice, earth, rock, or other material that flows quickly down the side of a mountain

caldera   a huge crater that forms when a stratovolcano caves in following an explosion

cinder cone   a steep-sided volcano made of cooled bits of lava called cinders

dormant   used to describe a volcano that hasn't erupted in the past 10,000 years but might erupt in the future

Earth's crust   the Earth's hard outer layer, or shell

earthquake   a shaking on the Earth's surface

extinct   used to describe a volcano that hasn't erupted for over 10,000 years and is unlikely to erupt ever again

fumarole   a hole in the ground around a volcano which allows steam and gas to escape

geothermal   the heat inside the earth

geyser   a spring near a volcano that shoots out jets of water and steam

lava   hot, melted rock that comes out of a volcano

lava bomb   lava that has exploded out of a volcano and dried midair to form a rock

magma   hot, melted rock that is below the Earth's surface

mudflow   a moving mass of liquid mud and rock that often follows a volcanic eruption

natural disaster   a major event caused by the natural processes of the Earth, such as an erupting volcano or an earthquake, that can cause damage and loss of life

renewable energy   energy made from natural resources such as wind, water, and sunshine

shield   a type of volcano in the shape of a warrior's shield, with gently sloping sides

stratovolcano   a type of volcano with steep sides made of many layers of lava and ash

supervolcano   enormous volcanoes that have eruptions a thousand times greater than other volcanoes

tectonic plates   the large, slow-moving pieces of the Earth's crust

tsunami   a giant wave that is often created by a volcanic eruption or earthquake

vent   an opening in the Earth's crust that allows lava, ash, rock, and gas to escape

INDEX